Tc
and the
Tornado

by Darleen Ramos
Illustrated by Anni Matsick

Glenview, Illinois • Boston, Massachusetts • Chandler, Arizona
Upper Saddle River, New Jersey

storm cellar

clouds

Tommy lived on a farm. He liked to fish. He liked to play with his dog, Tex.

One day, Christopher had to babysit Tommy. Christopher was Tommy's older brother.

"I can take care of myself!" Tommy said.

barn

cornfield

The boys went outside. It was a great day. The clouds were as white as snow. Tommy wanted to fish.

"Let's look for Granddad's old tools," Christopher said.

Tommy liked that idea. The boys ran to the barn. Tex followed them.

Extend Language **Simile**

As white as snow is a simile. Similes compare two things using the words *like* or *as*. Read the two similes below. Use each one in a sentence.

- as strong as a bull
- as quiet as a mouse

Christopher opened the barn door. The boys went up into the hayloft. Tex stayed below. The hayloft was dark and dusty. Tommy bumped into an old box.

"What is in here?" Tommy asked.

hayloft

picture

hay

The boys opened the box. They found old pictures.

Suddenly, Tex started barking. He was looking outside. Tommy opened the barn door.

The clouds were dark now! The sky was green! The boys knew these signs. A tornado was coming! They knew it would start to rain or hail soon.

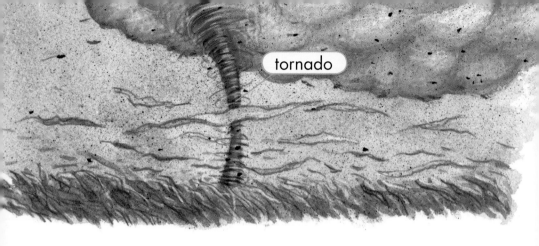

tornado

The boys ran to the storm cellar. The tornado was coming fast! Everything was flying around! It was dangerous outside. Suddenly, Christopher fell. He hurt his ankle. "Help me!" he yelled.

"I will help you!" Tommy shouted. "Let's go!"

Extend Language   **Word Ending *-ous***

The word ending *-ous* means "full of." *Dangerous* means "full of danger."

storm cellar

The tornado was as loud as a train. The wind threw branches. It blew dirt all around.

The boys and Tex got to the storm cellar. They went down the steps and shut the door. It was dark inside. The boys turned on a flashlight.

Did You Know? **Storm Cellars**

- A storm cellar is a safe place under the ground.
- People go there during a storm.
- Storm cellars usually have a wooden door and steps.
- People keep flashlights, blankets, and water inside them.

The tornado ended quickly. Tommy helped his
brother to the house.

Soon, their parents came home. They looked
worried. Then they saw the boys were safe.

"I was going to take care of Tommy," Christopher
said. "But he took care of me!"

"Way to go, Tommy!" his parents said.

Talk About It

1. What signs showed that a tornado was coming?
2. How did Tommy take care of Christopher?

Write About It

3. Draw a picture of any kind of big storm. Write one thing you should do to stay safe in a storm.

Extend Language

The ending -ous means "full of." The ending -ful also means "full of."

Draw this chart on a separate sheet of paper. Write the words that fit the meanings. Use the words at the top of the chart.

faithful   painful   beautiful   joyful

Meaning	Word with -ful
full of beauty	beautiful
full of joy	
full of pain	
full of faith	

ISBN-13: 978-0-328-49964-9
ISBN-10:   0-328-49964-1

6 7 8 9 10   V0FL   17 16 15 14 13

E L D Reader

Social Studies

Genre	Build Background	Access Content	Extend Language
Fiction	• Courage • Tornadoes • Power of Nature	• Fact Box • Labels	• Similes • Suffix *-ous*

Scott Foresman Reading Street 5.1.2

Scott Foresman
is an imprint of

ISBN-13: 978-0-328-49964-9
ISBN-10: 0-328-49964-1

9 780328 499649

90000